GARDEN PLANTS

VALUABLE TO BEES

by

INTERNATIONAL BEE RESEARCH ASSOCIATION

Principal collaborators

Mary F. Mountain, MSc, DipLA
Rosemary Day, BSc (IBRA)
Christine Quartley, PhD (BSBI)
Alison Goatcher (RHS)

International Bee Research Association

London
1981

published by International Bee Research Association

Registered office at the offices of
The Zoological Society of London,
Regent's Park,
London NW1, England

British Library Cataloguing in Publication Data
Garden plants valuable to bees
1. Honey plants
I. International Bee Research Association
635.9   SF535

ISBN 0-8609-8104-5

obtainable from:

International Bee Research Association,
Hill House, Gerrards Cross,
Bucks. SL9 ONR, England

Printed by Wotton Graphics (Chilterns) Ltd,
357 Uxbridge Road, Rickmansworth, Herts., England

3

CONTENTS

Preface   5

Information about the tables   7

TABLES

   Herbaceous plants   9

   Plants for the rock garden   16

   Culinary and aromatic herbs   18

   Bulbs, corms and tubers   20

   Annual and biennial plants   23

   Plants for the wild garden   27

   Climbers   34

   Trees   36

   Shrubs   41

Reading list   52

The cover shows an allegorical design based on beekeeping, taken from an engraving on copper by Carl August Grossmann (c. 1770)

As well as the skep and bees, and the flowers and branches of trees, there are symbols of human activities connected with honey and beeswax:
for gardening, a sickle, line and calipers
for agriculture, a scythe and a sheaf of corn
for painting, a palette
for medicine, the staff and entwined snakes of Aesculapius.

From the collection of Dr K.A. Forster.

PREFACE

There are books about garden plants for birds, and for butterflies, and here at last is one on garden plants for bees. More than any other member of the animal kingdom, bees can enrich our gardens. Not only does their contented hum have a pleasant sound; watching their foraging behaviour is a source of endless pleasure to bee lovers. If we can attract bees into our ornamental gardens, they will pollinate the fruit in our kitchen gardens, and we shall get larger crops and more perfectly formed fruits.

If we put a hive or two of bees into our own gardens we shall get a honey crop too. Bees often fly several kilometres to collect the nectar that they make into honey, which comes from plants in an area of several hundred hectares or acres. The honey is derived not so much from the garden plants as from more massive flowerings - of a lime tree avenue, a long hawthorn hedge, or a wilderness full of brambles and willowherb. Pollen provides protein needed for rearing the next generation of bees.

The importance of garden plants yielding nectar and pollen is that together they provide a continuous food supply, from willows and crocuses in early spring to ivy in late autumn. Colonies of bees need food all through the active season, so that they can develop and rear new bees that will collect the harvests when they come - perhaps during a week or two in May, and rather longer in July. This continuous food supply used to be provided by pastures that came into flower before they were cut, by verges and hedgerows, and by abundant weeds. Nowadays the efficiency of agriculture has greatly reduced these resources for the bees. But gardens designed for ease of management are most valuable in providing day-to-day food supplies that the countryside no longer yields. This provision is especially valuable in what beekeepers refer to as the June gap, when there is often a lull in the intensity of flowering.

The garden plants selected for inclusion in this book are not only valuable to bees: they are worth growing in their own right, and have been chosen for their horticultural merit.

The booklet "Trees and shrubs valuable to bees" by M. F. Mountain was published in 1965 and again in 1975. Its wide use led to many requests for a similar publication on other garden plants, which this book now provides. Since "Trees and shrubs" is again out of print, the material from it has been incorporated into the final three sections of the present book: climbers, trees, and shrubs. Entries in the first six sections, which comprise the major contents, were obtained as follows. They were initially drafted by Miss Mountain, then sent to nine experienced beekeeper/gardeners in different parts of England, who recorded their own observations during two seasons (1979, 1980). At IBRA the total information was co-ordinated by Rosemary Day, and Judith Dolby prepared the camera-ready copy. Botanical names were validated by Dr. Christine Quartley on behalf of the Botanical Society of the British Isles, and cultural details were supplied by Alison Goatcher at the Royal Horticultural Society.

The nine beekeeper/gardeners who worked as observers in 1979 and 1980 were: Mildred D. Bindley and David Charles, Somerset; Arthur G. Eames, Derbyshire; Dr. I. Keith Ferguson (Kew), Surrey; R. O. M. Page, Dorset; R. M. Payne, Avon; Rev. Patrick Rowley, South Yorkshire; Betty M. Showler, Bucks.; Ken Stevens, Devon. We are most grateful to all of them, as well as to the principal collaborators listed in the title page, for their work.

Eva Crane, Director
International Bee Research Association

INFORMATION ABOUT THE TABLES

The lists exclude most crop plants, most fruits, and all very invasive plants that are difficult to control. Where single and double flowered cultivars of a plant are available, single flowered cultivars are indicated, since these are more useful to bees.

The lists are designed for Britain and Ireland, and also for neighbouring parts of continental Europe: especially Denmark, Belgium, France, Germany, and the Netherlands. The flowering season listed is that for southern England in a "normal" year. "Ordinary garden soil" is neither too acid nor too alkaline (pH 5-7), and contains some humus-forming material.

Under "Notes" the order of entries is usually: description of plant (form of plant/leaves; arrangement, individual shape, colour, perfume of flowers); cultural requirements (soil type, moisture/drainage; aspect, sun/shade); other points of interest. The following abbreviations are used:

cv(s)	cultivar (cultivated variety)		
esp	especially	lv(s)	leaf, leaves
ev	evergreen	posn(s)	position(s)
fl(s)	flower(s), flowering	spp	species
fr(s)	fruit(s)	/	or

The height of plants is given in feet (ft or ') or inches (") and, in a well separated column, in metres (m); 1 ft = 12 inches; 1 m = 100 cm.

The final column shows the value of the plant to bees (meaning honeybees, hive bees); N and P indicate that they collect nectar and pollen, respectively. Plants especially used by bumble bees are marked B. The absence of all three entries (N, P, B) for a few plants reflects insufficiency of observations as to what it is that bees collect from the plant.   Garden plants are not normally a source of honey-dew, and no records are included here of its collection by bees.

The wild garden is regarded as any area planned to provide - with minimal maintenance - a succession of flowers, and other sources of interest and attraction, that are not suitable for the cultivated garden.   Some of the plants listed for the wild garden are useful to birds or butterflies as well as to bees, and a few are escapes and volunteer crop plants.   Most entries here would be regarded as weeds outside the wild garden.

Climbers, trees and shrubs are deciduous unless designated evergreen.   Climbers are not free-standing and require support.   All other plants with a trunk are grouped under trees.   It is unwise to plant trees listed as growing to a height of 30 ft (10 m) or more, unless the garden is a spacious one.   If the spread of a tree or shrub differs greatly from its height, this is indicated in the notes.

HERBACEOUS PLANTS

Botanical name	Common name	Flowers	Height ft	Notes	Height m	Value
Acanthus	bear's breeches	Jul–Aug	3–4	spectacular form with bracts and fls; sun/light shade	0.9–1.2	B
Achillea	yarrow	Jul–Aug	4"–4	many spp and cvs; well-drained soil, sun	0.1–1.2	N B
Anchusa azurea	large blue alkanet	Jun–Aug	3–5	several cvs, fls bright blue; fertile well-drained soil, sun	0.9–1.5	N B
Anthemis tinctoria	ox-eye chamomile, yellow chamomile	Jun–Aug	2½	many hybrids with A. sancti-johannis; well-drained soil, sun	0.8	N B
Armeria	thrift	May–Aug	2"–2	pink/red/white fls; well-drained soil, full sun	0.05–0.6	N P B
Aster	Michaelmas daisy			daisy-like fls; fertile soil, sun		N P
A. amellus	Michaelmas daisy	Aug–Sep	1½–2	several cvs, lavender/pink/rose fls	0.5–0.6	N P
A. novae-angliae	Michaelmas daisy	Sep–Oct	4–5	several cvs, pink/lavender fls	1.2–1.5	N P
A. novi-belgii	Michaelmas daisy	Sep–Oct	9"–4'	many cvs, wide range of shades	0.23–1.2	N P
A. sedifolius = A. acris	Michaelmas daisy	Aug–Sep	2–2½	lavender-blue fls	0.6–0.8	N P
Caltha palustris	marsh marigold	Feb–Jan	1–1½	profuse cup-shaped yellow-golden fls; water up to 6" deep/loamy moist soil	0.3–0.5	N P B

Botanical name	Common name	Flowers	Height ft	Notes	Height m	Value
Campanula lactiflora	milky bellflower	Jun-Jul	3-5	several cvs, lavender-blue bell-shaped fls; fertile well-drained soil	0.9-1.5	N P
C. persicifolia	peach-leaved bellflower	Jul	1-3	white/blue/purple fls; well-drained fertile soil, dead-head the fls	0.3-0.9	N P
Centaurea montana	perennial cornflower	Jun	1½-2	blue fls, other cvs with white/pink fls; fertile well-drained soil, sun	0.5-0.6	N B
Chrysanthemum	Korean chrysanthemum	Oct	<3	many shades; fertile well-drained soil, some lime, sun	<0.9	P
C. coccineum (single cvs)	pyrethrum	May-Jun	<3	wide range of shades; well-drained soil, sun	<0.9	P
C. maximum = Leucanthemum maximum	Shasta daisy	Jun-Aug	2½-3	single white fls; fertile well-drained soil preferably with lime, sun	0.8-0.9	B
Cichorium intybus	chicory	Jul-Oct	<3	sky-blue dandelion-like fls, also pink cv; fertile soil with some lime, hearted head of lvs used in salads	<0.9	N P B
Coreopsis grandiflora	coreopsis	Jul-Aug	1-1½	several cvs, bright yellow fls; well-drained soil, stake plants early on	0.3-0.5	N P
C. verticillata		Jun-Sep	1½-2	fern-like lvs, yellow fls; well-drained soil, does not need staking	0.5-0.6	N P

Botanical name	Common name	Flowering		Description	Height (m)	N P B
Cynara scolymus	globe artichoke	Jun–Sep	<5	very decorative, edible fl heads; well-drained fertile soil, shelter, sun	<1.5	B
Dictamnus albus = D. fraxinella	burning bush	Jun–Jul	2	aromatic plant, white/pink/red fls; well-drained soil preferably with lime, sun	0.6	N P
Doronicum plantagineum	leopard's-bane	Mar–Apr	2	golden-yellow fls; deep moist soil, sun/pt shade	0.6	N P B
Echinops ritro	globe thistle	Aug	3–4	steel-blue fls to dry for indoor decoration; well-drained soil, sun	0.9–1.2	N B
Erigeron	fleabane	Jun–Aug	3"–2'	several spp and cvs, daisy-like fls in many shades; moist well-drained soil, sun	0.08–0.6	N B
Eryngium maritimum	sea holly	Jul–Sep	1–1½	cone-shaped metallic blue fls suitable for drying; well-drained soil, sun	0.3–0.5	N B
E. tripartitum		Jul–Sep	2½	grey-blue globular fls; well-drained soil, sun, needs staking	0.8	N B
Eupatorium		Jul–Sep	2–6	white/red/purple/pink fls; moist soil, sun/pt shade	0.6–1.8	N P
Gaillardia hybrids	blanket flower	Jun–Oct	2–2½	yellow and red daisy-like fls; light well-drained soil, sun	0.6–0.8	N P
Geranium ibericum		Jun–Aug	1½–2	violet-blue fls; well-drained soil, sun/pt shade	0.5–0.6	N
G. phaeum	dusky cranesbill, mourning widow	Jun–Jul	2	dark maroon fls, cvs with white fls; tolerates deep shade	0.6	N

Botanical name	Common name	Flowers	Height ft	Notes	Height m	Value
G. pratense	meadow cranesbill	Jul-Sep	1½-2	blue/violet-blue fls, other cvs white/light blue; well-drained soil, sun/pt shade	0.5-0.6	N
Geum	avens	May-Jun	½-2	many spp, long lasting bright coloured fls; ordinary garden soil, sun/pt shade	0.15-0.6	P
Gypsophila paniculata (single cvs)	baby's breath	Jul-Aug	3	numerous tiny white fls; well-drained soil, sun	0.9	N
Helenium	sneezeweed	Jul-Aug	4-6	many hybrids and cvs, yellow/red/orange fls; ordinary soil, sun	1.2-1.8	N P B
Helianthus	sunflower	Jul-Oct	3-10	yellow fls; well-drained soil, sun	0.9-3.0	N P
Helleborus	Christmas rose, Lenten rose, hellebore	Dec-Mar	1-2	white/green/purple fls; well-drained but moist soil several spp like shade	0.3-0.6	N
Heuchera	coral flower	Jun-Sep	1-1½	many hybrids and cvs, tiny red/pink/white fls; light well-drained soil, sun/pt shade	0.3-0.5	N
Impatiens noli-tangere	touch-me-not	Aug-Sep	1½	yellow fls spotted with red inside; moist soil	0.5	N P B
Iris unguicularis = I. stylosa	Algerian iris	Oct-Mar	9"	fls soft lavender with a yellow blaze on falls; well-drained soil, sun	0.23	N
Liatris spicata	blazing star, gay feather	Sep	2-3	pink-purple fls, tuberous roots; ordinary soil, sun	0.6-0.9	N

Botanical name	Common name	Height (m)	Type	Flowering	No.
Ligularia dentata = Senecio clivorum		clusters of orange-yellow fls; ordinary soil, preferably moist — 0.9-1.5 — N P		Jul-Aug	3-5
Limonium	sea lavender, statice	lavender blue/pink/purple fls suitable for drying; well-drained soil, sun — 0.3-0.6 — N		Jul-Sep	1-2
Lobelia cardinalis	cardinal lobelia, cardinal flower	scarlet fls; rich moist soil, pt shade, shelter, winter protection — 0.8 — B		Jul-Aug	2½
Lupinus	lupin	many small fls in colourful spire-like racemes; neutral-acid soil, sun/pt shade — 0.9-1.5 — P B		May-Jul	3-5
Lysimachia vulgaris	yellow loosestrife	yellow fls; moist soil, shade — 0.6-0.9 — P B		Jul-Sep	2-3
Monarda didyma	sweet bergamot, bee balm, Oswego tea	scarlet/purple/pink/white fls; aromatic lvs can be used in tea; moist soil, sun/pt shade — 0.6-0.9 — B		Jun-Sep	2-3
Nepeta x faassenii = N. mussinii	catmint	spikes of lavender-blue fls; well-drained soil, sun/pt shade — 0.3-0.5 — N		Jun-Aug	1-1½
Oenothera	evening-primrose	slightly scented yellow fls; well-drained soil, sun — 0.3-1.2 — P		Jun-Sep	1-4
Paeonia (single cvs)	paeony	handsome white/yellow/pink/red fls; moist but well-drained soil, sun/pt shade, resents root disturbance — 0.5-1.8 — P B		May-Jun	1½-6
Papaver orientale	oriental poppy	large scarlet fls, cvs with pink/white fls; well-drained soil, sun — 0.6-0.9 — P B		May-Jun	2-3
Penstemon		many hybrids, scarlet/rose/purple fls; well-drained soil, full sun — 0.3-0.6 — N B		Jun-Jul	1-2

Botanical name	Common name	Flowers	Height ft	Notes	Height m	Value
Polemonium caeruleum	Jacob's ladder, Greek valerian	Apr-Jul	1-2	blue/white fls; rich soil, sun/pt shade	0.3-0.6	N P
Polygonatum x hybridum	Solomon's seal, David's harp	May-Jun	2-4	attractive form, white fls; almost any type of soil, sunny posn	0.6-1.2	N B
Polygonum affine		Jun-Sep	6"-9"	red fls; ordinary soil, sun, can be very invasive	0.15-0.23	N
P. amplexicaule		Jun on	3-4	free-flowering, red fls; rich moist soil, sun/pt shade	0.9-1.2	N P
P. campanulatum		Jun-Sep	2½-3½	shell-pink fls; rich moist soil, light shade, cut fl stems to ground level in Oct	0.8-1.1	N
Primula vulgaris elatior	polyanthus	Apr-May	5"-9"	many different colours; fertile moist garden soil, sun/pt shade	0.13-0.23	B
Pulmonaria saccharata	soldiers & sailors, lungwort	Mar-Apr	1	fls open pink and change to sky-blue; damp soil, shade	0.3	B
Rudbeckia	coneflower	Jul on	1-7	fls orange/yellow/rust; well-drained soil, sun	0.3-2.1	N B
R. laciniata	coneflower	Aug-Sep	6-7	yellow fls, green central cone; well-drained soil, sun	1.8-2.1	N
Salvia x superba = S. virgata nemorosa		Jun-Sep	2	purple-blue fls; well-drained soil, sun	0.6	N
Scabiosa	scabious	Jun-Sep	1½-2	lavender-blue fls, several cvs; fertile well-drained soil, sun	0.5-0.6	N

Botanical name	Common name	Flowering	Height	Description	(m)	Type
Sedum spectabile		Sep-Oct	1-1½	rose/pink fls; well-drained soil, sun	0.3-0.5	N
Sidalcea	sidalcea	Jun-Sep	2½-4½	several cvs, spikes of pink fls; ordinary soil, sun	0.8-1.8	N
Solidago	golden-rod	Jul-Oct	½-6	many spp and cvs, yellow fls; any soil type, sun/pt shade	0.15-1.8	N P
Stachys	woundwort	Jul-Sep	½-1	purple fls; well-drained soil, sun/pt shade	0.15-0.3	N B
S. lanata = S. byzantina	lamb's ear, lamb's tongue	Jul	1-1½	silver lvs, purple fls; well-drained soil, sun/pt shade, may not survive in cold wet seasons, ground cover	0.3-0.5	N
Thalictrum	meadow-rue	Apr-Aug	1-5	many spp, attractive lvs, small fluffy fls; rich moist soil, sun/light shade	0.3-1.5	P B
Verbascum	mullein	Jun-Sep	3	long spikes of yellow fls; ordinary soil, full sun	0.9	N P B
Veronica spicata	spiked speedwell	Jun-Aug	½-1½	racemes of blue fls, several cvs; well-drained but not dry soil	0.15-0.5	N P

PLANTS FOR THE ROCK GARDEN

Botanical name	Common name	Flowers	Height ft	Notes	Height m	Value
Alyssum saxatile	golden alyssum	Apr–May	9"–1	golden-yellow fls; well-drained soil, full sun	0.23–0.3	N P
Arabis caucasica =A. albida	white arabis, garden rockcress	Feb–Jun	9"	white fls; well-drained soil, pt shade, very invasive	0.23	N P
Aster alpinus		Jul	6"	purple-blue daisy-like fls, cvs in other shades; fertile soil, sun	0.15	N P
Aubrieta deltoidea	aubrieta	Mar–Apr	3"–4"	purple fls, several cvs; well-drained soil, likes lime, sun	0.08–0.10	N P B
Campanula carpatica	Carpathian harebell	Jun	9"–1	blue/purple/white cup-shaped fls; fertile well-drained soil, sun/pt shade	0.23–0.3	N P B
Carpobrotus edulis = Mesembryanthemum edule	Hottentot fig	Jun–Jul	3"	fleshy lvs, showy mauve fls; well-drained soil, good by coast, stands salt spray	0.08	N P
Geranium sanguineum lancastriense	bloody cranesbill	Jun–Sep	3"–4"	pink fls with dark veins, other cvs; ordinary well-drained soil, sun/pt shade	0.08–0.10	N P
Gypsophila repens		Jun–Aug	6"	greyish lvs, small white/pink fls; well-drained soil with some lime, sun	0.15	N
Helianthemum nummularium	rock-rose	Jun–Jul	3"–1	yellow/orange/red/pink/white fls; ordinary well-drained soil, sun, invasive	0.08–0.3	P B

Name	Common name	Flowering	Height	Description		
Hypericum olympicum		Jun–Aug	9"–1	yellow fls; fertile well-drained soil, sun	0.23–0.3	P B
Lithospermum			4"–15"	funnel-shaped blue fls; sandy soil with peat/leaf mould, no lime, full sun	0.10–0.4	N
Lobularia maritima = Alyssum maritimum	sweet alyssum	Jun–Sep	3"–6"	white/purple/lilac fls; ordinary well-drained soil, full sun	0.08–0.15	P
Saxifraga	saxifrage			many spp; most need sharply drained soil with lime and grit		N P
Sedum	stonecrop		1"–6"	many spp; numerous small star-shaped pink/yellow/white fls; well-drained soil, full sun	0.03–0.15	N P B
S. spurium		Jul	4"	mat-forming plant, rich pink fls; well-drained soil, full sun	0.10	N
Thymus	thyme	Jun	1"–9"	several spp, small aromatic lvs variegated cvs, white/pink/lilac fls; well-drained soil, sun	0.03–0.23	N B
Veronica teucrium		Jun–Aug	9"–1½	sky-blue fls; well-drained soil, sun	0.23–0.5	N

CULINARY AND AROMATIC HERBS

Botanical name	Common name	Flowers	Height ft	Notes	Height m	Value
Agastache foeniculum = A. anethiodora	anise hyssop	Jun–Sep	1½	aromatic lvs used in cooking/ pot-pourri, blue fls; ordinary well-drained soil, sunny posn	0.5	N
Allium schoenoprasum	chives	Jun–Jul	6"–10"	lvs used in cookery, pink fls; loamy soil, sun/semi-shade	0.15–0.25	N P
Borago officinalis	borage	May–Aug	1–2	edible lvs and blue fls; well-drained soil, sun	0.3–0.6	N P B
Marrubium vulgare	white horehound	Jul–Sep	1–2	medicinal herb, downy stems and lvs, fls in white whorls; poor soil	0.3–0.6	N
Mentha	mint	Jul–Sep	1–3	many spp, aromatic perennial used in cooking/pot pourri; best in rich moist soil, shelter and part shade	0.3–0.9	N
Ocimum basilicum	basil	Aug	2–3	aromatic lvs, used in cooking small white fls; warm posn	0.6–0.9	N
Origanum marjorana	knotted marjoram, sweet marjoram	Jul–Sep	1	aromatic lvs, used in cooking, white/mauve/pink fls; grow as an annual in well-drained soil, sunny posn	0.3	N
O. onites	perennial marjoram, pot marjoram	Jul–Sep	2	aromatic lvs, pink/white fls; warm well-drained soil, shelter	0.6	N
O. vulgare	wild marjoram	Jul–Sep	1–2	aromatic lvs, pink fls; well-drained calcareous soil, sun	0.3–0.6	N P B

Latin name	Common name	Flowering		Description			
Salvia officinalis	sage	Jun–Jul	2	aromatic lvs, used in cooking, purple/white fls; light well-drained soil, sun, shelter	0.6	N	
Satureia	savory	Jul–Oct	1	aromatic lvs, used in cooking, rose/white fls; well-drained soil, sunny posn	0.3	N	B
Thymus vulgaris	thyme	Jun	9"–1	aromatic lvs, used in cooking, mauve fls; well-drained soil, sun	0.23–0.3	N	B

BULBS, CORMS AND TUBERS

Botanical name	Common name	Flowers	Height ft	Notes	Height m	Value
Allium		Mar–Jul	½–4	onion-scented lvs, fls mauve/crimson/red/yellow globular heads; well-drained soil, sun	0.15–1.2	N P
Anemone blanda		Feb–Apr	½	blue/mauve/pink/white fls; well-drained soil, sun/pt shade	0.15	P B
Camassia	quamash	Jun–Jul	1–4	racemes of star-shaped white/blue/purple fls; heavy moist soil, dead-head fls, plant 3–4" deep	0.3–1.2	N P
Chionodoxa luciliae	glory of the snow	Feb–Apr	½	light-blue white-centred fls; well-drained soil, full sun, plant 3–4" deep	0.15	N P
Colchicum autumnale	meadow saffron	Aug–Sep	½	lilac/white/rose-pink fls; good in shrub borders/rough grass, plant 3–4" deep	0.15	N P B
Convallaria majalis	lily of the valley	May–Jun	6"–8"	rhizomes, scented white fls; add leaf mould/compost to soil, pt shade	0.15–0.20	P
Crocus		Feb–Mar	2"–5"	many spp, fls yellow/white/mauve/purple; well-drained soil, shelter from wind, plant 3" deep	0.05–0.13	N P
C. balansae		Mar	3"	orange fls	0.08	N P
C. chrysanthus		Feb–Mar	3"	golden-yellow fls, also cvs and hybrids in other colours	0.08	N P

Botanical name	Common name	Flowering	Height	Description	Height (m)	Uses
C. tomasinianus		Feb-Mar	3"	lilac/mauve fls	0.08	N P
Dahlia (single cvs)		Jul to frost	1½-2½	tuberous roots, bright coloured fls; well-drained soil with peat/compost, store tubers in frost-free posn	0.5-0.8	N P B
Eranthis hyemalis	winter aconite	Jan-Feb	4"	tuberous roots, lemon-yellow fls; moist well-drained loam, sun/pt shade, plant 1" deep	0.10	N P
Fritillaria imperialis	crown imperial	Apr	2-3	pendent clusters of yellow/red/orange fls; fertile well-drained soil, sun/pt shade, plant 8" deep	0.6-0.9	N B
F. meleagris	snake's head fritillary	Apr-May	1-1½	chequered white/pink/purple bell-shaped fls; moist soil, good in short turf, plant 4-6"	0.3-0.5	N P
Galanthus nivalis	common snowdrop	Feb-Mar	3"-8"	white fls with green markings; heavy moist loam, some shade	0.08-0.2	N P
Galtonia candicans	Cape hyacinth, summer hyacinth	Jul-Sep	4	bell-shaped white fls; plant 6" deep, leave undisturbed once established	1.2	N
Hyacinthella azurea = Hyacinthus azureus = Muscari azureum		Mar	3"-8"	spikes of pale blue fls; well-drained soil, pt shade, good on rock garden, plant 2-3" deep	0.08-0.2	P
Hyacinthus orientalis	hyacinth	Apr-May	6"-9"	hybrids in many shades, spikes of fragrant fls; plant bulbs 5-6" deep	0.15-0.23	N P
Leucojum vernum	spring snowflake	Mar-Apr	8"	white, green-tipped fls; moist conditions, some shade, plant bulbs 3-4" deep	0.20	N P

Botanical name	Common name	Flowers	Height ft	Notes	Height m	Value
Muscari botryoides	grape hyacinth	Mar–Apr	6"–8"	spikes of blue/white fls; ordinary well-drained soil, full sun, plant 3" deep	0.15–0.20	N P
Scilla sibirica		Mar–Apr	<6"	blue/white bell-shaped fls; moist well-drained soil, sun/pt shade, plant 2–3" deep	<0.15	N P
Tigridia pavonia	tiger flower	Jul–Sep	1½–2	many cvs, fls usually yellow spotted crimson-brown; well-drained but moist soil, warm posn, sun, plant 3–4" deep	0.5–0.6	N
Tulipa	tulip	Mar–May	6"–3'	fls goblet-shaped, many colours; alkaline soil, dead-head when petals fall, plant 6" deep	0.15–0.9	P
T. kaufmanniana	water-lily tulip	Mar	4"–10"	greyish lvs, white fls flushed red and yellow, many cvs of different colour; alkaline soil	0.10–0.25	P B

ANNUAL AND BIENNIAL PLANTS

Botanical name	Common name	Flowers	Height ft	Notes	Height m	Value
Alcea rosea = Althaea rosea	hollyhock	Jul–Sep	4½–9	tall spikes of fls, many colours; rich heavy soil, shelter, stake in exposed posns	1.4–2.7	N P B
Antirrhinum majus	snapdragon	Jul–Oct	1–4	spikes of fragrant fls, many colours; fertile light well-drained soil, sun	0.3–1.2	B
Begonia semperflorens	fibrous-rooted begonia	Jun–Sep	½–1	red/pink/white fls; light moist but well-drained soil, pt shade	0.15–0.3	P
Calendula officinalis (single cvs)	pot marigold	May–Oct	2	orange/yellow daisy-like fls, lvs and stems with pungent aroma; poor/well-drained soil, dead-head regularly	0.6	N P B
Campanula medium	Canterbury bell	May–Jul	1–3	white/blue/pink/violet bell-shaped fls; fertile well-drained soil, sun/pt shade	0.3–0.9	N P
Centaurea cyanus	cornflower	Jun–Sep	1–3	sprays of pink/red/purple/blue/ white fls; fertile well-drained soil, sun	0.3–0.9	N P
Cheiranthus	wallflower	May–Jun	½–2	freely produced fls, many shades; ordinary well-drained soil, sun, pinch out tips of young plants to encourage branching	0.15–0.6	N P B
Chrysanthemum parthenium = Tanacetum parthenium	feverfew	Jul–Sep	9"–1½	short-lived perennial, aromatic lvs, white/yellow fls; fertile light well-drained soil, sun	0.23–0.5	B

23

Botanical name	Common name	Flowers	Height ft	Notes	Height m	Value
Clarkia elegans (single cvs)	clarkia	Jul-Sep	1½-2	spikes of white/lavender/pink/rose fls; medium-light slightly acid loam, sun	0.5-0.6	N P
Cleome spinosa	spider flower	Jul	3-4	white/pink/yellow fls; fertile well-drained soil, full sun	0.9-1.2	N
Convolvulus tricolor = C. minor		Jul-Sep	1-1½	blue/cinnamon/crimson fls; ordinary well-drained soil, sun, dead-head regularly	0.3-0.5	N P B
Cosmos bipinnatus	cosmos	Aug-Sep	<3	white/pink/rose daisy fls; free flowering; light poor soil, sun	<0.9	N
Cucurbita pepo	ornamental gourds	Jul-Sep		large yellow fls, ornamental frs; ordinary, well-drained soil, train up trellis/trailing		N P B
Dianthus barbatus	sweet William	Jun-Jul	1-2	scented fls, many colours; ordinary well-drained soil, sun	0.3-0.6	N B
Echium plantagineum = E. lycopsis	purple viper's bugloss	Jun-Aug	3	blue/purple fls; light dry soil, open posn, sun	0.9	N P
Eschscholzia californica	Californian poppy	Jun-Oct	1-1½	orange-yellow, saucer-shaped fls; poor sandy soils, sun	0.3-0.5	N P B
Gaillardia		Jul-Oct	1½-2½	bright yellow and orange fls; light, well-drained soil	0.5-0.8	N P
Gilia capitata		Jun-Sep	1½	lavender-blue pincushion fl head; light well-drained soil, full sun	0.5	N P
Godetia (single cvs)		Jun-Aug	1-2	spikes/clusters of funnel-shaped fls; light moist soil, sun	0.3-0.6	N P

Botanical name	Common name	Flowering	Spacing	Description	Height (m)	Type
Gypsophila elegans		May-Sep	2	numerous small white/pink/rose fls; well-drained soil, sun	0.6	N
Helianthus annuus	annual sunflower	Jul-Aug	3-10	huge yellow/copper bronze fls; well-drained soil, sun	0.9-3.0	N P B
Heliotropium x hybridum		Aug	1-2	small violet/lavender/white fls; fertile well-drained soil, sun	0.3-0.6	N B
Iberis umbellata	annual candytuft	Jul	6"-15"	small white/pink/purple fl heads; well-drained soil, sun	0.15-0.4	N P
Impatiens glandulifera	Himalayan balsam	Aug-Sep	3-5	purple/yellow/rose fls; fertile well-drained moist soil, sun/pt shade	0.9-1.5	N P
Lavatera trimestris = L. rosea	mallow	Jul-Sep	2-3	rose-pink fls; ordinary soil, shelter, sun	0.6-0.9	N P
Limnanthes douglasii	poached-egg flower	May-Jun	½	yellow and white scented fls; open sunny posn and cool root run – by paths/between rocks/paving	0.15	N P B
Limonium sinuatum = Statice sinuata	statice	Jul	1½	fls dried for decoration, many shades; well-drained soil, open posn, sun	0.5	N
Linum	flax	Jun-Aug	1½-2	rose/blue fls; well-drained soil, sun	0.5-0.6	N P
Lobelia erinus	lobelia	May on	4"-9"	blue/white/pink fls; rich moist soil, pt shade, also trailing cvs	0.10-0.23	N
Lunaria annua = L. biennis	honesty	Apr-May	2½	fragrant purple fls, silvery seed pods for indoor decoration; light soil, pt shade	0.8	N P
Myosotis	forget-me-not	Apr-May	3"-8"	small blue fragrant fls; loamy soil, pt shade	0.08-0.2	N P B

Botanical name	Common name	Flowers	Height ft	Notes	Height m	Value
Nemophila menziesii = N. insignis	baby blue eyes	Jun	6"-9"	white centred sky-blue fls; moist soil, sun/pt shade	0.15-0.23	N
Nicotiana	tobacco plant	Jun-Sep	2-3	scented fls, many shades; rich well-drained soil, sun	0.6-0.9	N P B
Nigella damascena	love-in-a-mist	Jun-Aug	2	attractive seed pods, blue/white fls; fertile soil, sun	0.6	N P
Oenothera biennis	common evening-primrose	Jun-Oct	3-4	large yellow fls; ordinary well-drained soil, sun	0.9-1.2	P
Papaver	poppy	Jun-Aug	1½-2½	fls in many shades; well-drained soil, sun	0.5-0.8	P
Phacelia campanularia		Jun-Sep	9"	lvs fragrant when crushed, blue fls; sandy well-drained soil, sun	0.23	N P
P. tanacetifolia	tansy phacelia	Jul-Aug	2	lavender fls; fertile moist soil, sun	0.6	N P
Reseda odorata	mignonette	Jun-Oct	1½-2	scented yellowish heads of small fls; rich, well-drained alkaline soil, sun	0.5-0.6	N P B
Salvia horminum		Jun-Sep	1½	coloured bracts, fls can be dried; well-drained soil, sun	0.5	B
Ursinia anethoides		Jun-Sep	1½	colourful orange daisy-like fls; sandy soil, sun	0.5	P
Zinnia elegans (single cvs)		Jul-Sep	2-2½	daisy-like fls, many colours, suitable for cutting/bedding; rich well-drained soil, shelter, sun	0.6-0.8	N P

PLANTS FOR THE WILD GARDEN

Botanical name	Common name	Flowers	Height ft	Notes	Height m	Value
Agrostemma githago	corn cockle	Jun-Sep	1-3	purple fls; rare annual weed, once common in cornfields	0.3-0.9	P
Allium ursinum	ramsons	Apr-Jun	1	plant smells strongly of onion, white fls; damp, shady areas	0.3	N
Anchusa officinalis	alkanet	Jun-Aug	1-2	branched hairy perennial, purple fls; fields/waysides etc	0.3-0.6	N
Anemone nemorosa	wood anemone	Mar-May	3"-6"	nodding, solitary white fls with pink or purplish tinge; woods/ hedgerows	0.08-0.15	P B
Arctium	burdock	Jul-Sep	2½-4	downy biennial, purple thistle-like fls; hooked fruits, waste ground/dry woods	0.8-1.2	N P B
Asparagus officinalis	asparagus	Jun-Aug	4-5	fern-like lvs, tiny greenish fls; well-drained soil with compost	1.2-1.5	N P B
Barbarea vulgaris	winter cress	May-Jun	1-2	mustard-like perennial, dark shining lvs, yellow fls; stream banks/roadsides	0.3-0.6	N P B
Brassica				many spp esp crop plants if left to seed, e.g. cabbage, turnip, rape, mustard, etc		N P
Campanula glomerata	clustered bellflower	May-Sep	6"-8"	stiff, hairy perennial, clusters of violet fls; dry chalky fields	0.15-0.2	N P

Botanical name	Common name	Flowers	Height ft	Notes	Height m	Value
Centaurea	knapweed, hardheads	Jul-Sep	1-2	purple thistle-like fls; rough grass/banks	0.3-0.6	N P B
Chrysanthemum vulgare = Tanacetum vulgare	tansy	Jul-Sep	1-3	attractive aromatic lvs, yellow button-like fls; waste places	0.3-0.9	N P B
Cirsium	thistle	Jun on	1-5	prickly lvs, purple/pink/ lilac fls; fields/roadsides, very invasive	0.3-1.5	N P B
Clematis vitalba	old man's beard, traveller's joy	Jul		rope-like stems, climber, cream fls; calcareous soil, hedges/ woods		N P B
Cynoglossum officinale	houndstongue	Jun-Aug	1-2	downy grey perennial, purple/ red fls, hooked fruits; dry soil/sand-dunes	0.3-0.6	N P B
Daucus carota	wild carrot	Jun on	1-2	rough hairy biennial, feathery lvs, fls in whitish umbels; grassy places, alkaline soil	0.3-0.6	N P
Dipsacus fullonum	teasel	Jul-Sep	6	prickly biennial, conical lilac fl head with spines, standing through winter on dead stems; rough grass	1.8	N B
Echium vulgare	viper's bugloss	Jun-Sep	1-3	rough hairy biennial, fls vivid blue with pink buds; chalky/light dry soils, often near sea	0.3-0.9	N P B
Epilobium angustifolium	fireweed, rosebay willowherb	Jul-Sep	5	rampant perennial, pink-purple fl spikes; troublesome weed producing many seeds, woods/waste places	1.5	N P B

Scientific name	Common name	Flowering		Description	Height (m)	
E. hirsutum	great hairy willowherb	Jul-Aug	6	our tallest willowherb, pink fls; damp areas	1.8	N P B
Eupatorium cannabinum	hemp agrimony	Jul-Aug	4	mauve/reddish/white fl heads; damp woodland/marshy soil	1.2	N P
Fagopyrum esculentum	buckwheat, brank	Jul-Aug	1-2	hairless annual, stems often reddish, pink/white fls; not native, crop plant found as an escape	0.3-0.6	N P
Filipendula ulmaria = Spiraea ulmaria	meadowsweet	Jun-Sep	2-4	stiff hairless perennial, many white/cream fls; damp meadows/woods	0.6-1.2	P
Foeniculum vulgare	fennel	Jul on	3-5	strong-smelling perennial, feathery-lvs, fls in yellow umbels; waste land/near sea	0.9-1.5	N
Glechoma hederacea	ground ivy	Mar-Jun	4"	perennial, rooting runners, violet-blue fls; hedges/ waste ground/woods	0.1	N P B
Heracleum sphondylium	hogweed	Jun on	2-4	coarse hairy biennial, fls in large white/pink umbels; roadsides/grassy places	0.6-1.2	N P B
Hieracium	hawkweed	May-Oct	<4	hairy perennial, yellow/ orange-red dandelion-like fls; widespread	<1.2	N P B
Isatis tinctoria	woad	Jun-Aug	1½-3	biennial, many small yellow fls; fields/waste places, formerly cultivated for blue dye	0.5-0.9	N
Knautia arvensis	field scabious	Jun on	1-3	hairy perennial, flat heads of bluish-lilac fls; dry grassy places	0.3-0.9	N P B

Botanical name	Common name	Flowers	Height ft	Notes	Height m	Value
Lamium purpureum	red deadnettle	all year	3"–9"	purplish downy annual, dark pinkish-purple fls; weed of cultivated ground	0.08–0.23	N P B
Leontodon	hawkbit	Jun–Sep	¼–1½	yellow dandelion-like fls; grassy places	0.15–0.5	N P B
Leonurus cardiaca	motherwort	Jul on	2–4	fls light purple; poor soil	0.6–1.2	N
Linaria vulgaris	toadflax	Jul–Oct	9"–2'	perennial, yellow snapdragon-like fls; grassy banks/waste places, rampant	0.23–0.6	N P B
Lotus corniculatus	birdsfoot trefoil	May–Sep	<½	prostrate perennial, yellow/red pea-like fls; dry grass	<0.15	N P B
Lycopus europaeus	gipsywort	Jul–Sep	3	scentless, mint-like plant, whorls of white fls; wet places	0.9	N
Lythrum salicaria	purple loosestrife	Jun–Sep	3–4	perennial, whorls of red-purple fls; marshes/riversides	0.9–1.2	N P B
Malva	mallow	Jun on	1–3	coarse hairy perennials, pink-purple fls; waste ground	0.3–0.9	N P
Melilotus	melilot, sweet clover	Jun–Sep	4	hairless annuals/biennials, white/yellow vetch-like fls; fields/waste places	1.2	N P B
Nepeta cataria	wild catmint	Jul–Sep	2	minty scent, whorls of white fls spotted pink; hedge banks/ roadsides, quite rare	0.6	N
Onobrychis viciifolia	sainfoin	Jun–Aug	1–2	perennial, racemes of pink pea fls; dry chalk soil	0.3–0.6	N P

Scientific name	Common name	Flowering	Height	Description	Size (m)	N P B
Papaver rhoeas	field poppy	Jun on	9"-2'	hairy annual, scarlet fls; arable land/roadsides etc	0.23-0.6	N P B
Pastinaca sativa	wild parsnip	Jul-Sep	2-4	unpleasant smelling biennial, yellow fls; chalk grassland	0.6-1.2	N
Pentaglottis sempervirens = Anchusa sempervirens	evergreen alkanet, green alkanet	Apr-Jul	1-2	rough hairy perennial, small clusters of bright blue fls; shade	0.3-0.6	N
Petasites fragrans	winter heliotrope	Dec-Feb	6"-8"	rampant, creeping perennial, scented white/lilac fls; garden escape/waste places	0.15-0.2	N P
P. hybridus	butterburr	Mar-Apr	½-1	large rhubarb-like lvs, pinkish white fls; rivers/damp places	0.15-0.3	N P
Plantago lanceolata	ribwort plantain	Apr on	½-2	fls in dense ½-1" spikes, prominant anthers; lawns/waste places	0.15-0.6	P
Ranunculus ficaria	lesser celandine	Mar-May	3"	hairless perennial, yellow fls shiny petals; damp shade	0.08	P
Raphanus raphanistrum	white charlock, white radish	May on	½-1½	straggly annual, whitish fls; farm/garden weed	0.15-0.5	N P
Salvia verticillata	whorl-flowered clary	May-Aug	15"-2½	strong-smelling perennial, whorls of blue-violet fls; dry stony places	0.4-0.8	N
Saxifraga umbrosa	St Patrick's cabbage	Jun-Jul	½-1	rosettes of lvs, small whitish fls; rocky areas, London Pride is a hybrid form	0.15-0.3	N P
Scilla nonscripta	bluebell	Apr-Jun	1	bulbous perennial, fragrant blue fls; woods/hedge banks	0.3	N P

Botanical name	Common name	Flowers	Height ft	Notes	Height m	Value
Scrophularia aquatica	water figwort	Jun-Sep	2-4	small red-brown globular fls; wet places	0.6-1.2	N P B
S. nodosa	common figwort	Jun-Aug	2-3	hairless perennial, small red-brown fls; woods/damp shade	0.6-0.9	N P B
Sinapis arvensis	charlock	May-Jul	½-1½	bristly annual, yellow fls; agricultural weed	0.15-0.5	N P B
Solidago virgaurea	golden-rod	Jul-Sep	2½	golden-yellow fls; dry woods/dunes/heaths/hedge banks	0.8	N P
Sonchus	sow-thistle	May-Oct	3	dandelion-like fls; fields/waste places	0.9	N P
Symphytum asperum	rough comfrey	Jun on	2-4	our tallest comfrey, small usually blue fls; drier places	0.6-1.2	N P B
Taraxacum officinale	dandelion	Mar-Oct	2"-1	yellow daisy-like fls; grassy/waste places	0.05-0.3	N P B
Teucrium scorodonia	wood sage	Jul-Aug	1	inconspicuous greenish fls, maroon stamens; dry shade	0.3	N B
Thymus serpyllum	thyme	Jun	2"	aromatic carpeting perennial, reddish-purple fls; heaths/dunes	0.05	N P B
Trifolium pratense	red clover	May-Sep	4"-1½	perennial, sweetly scented pinkish-red fls; grassy areas	0.10-0.5	N P B
T. repens	white clover, Dutch clover	May-Oct	4"	low, creeping perennial, white/pinkish fls in round heads; grassy places	0.10	N P B

						N P B
Tussilago farfara	coltsfoot	Feb-Mar	3"-4"	low perennial, yellow fls; clay, bare/sparsely vegetated ground	0.08-0.10	N P B
Verbena officinalis	vervain	Jul-Sep	1½	wirey perennial, small lilac fls; waste ground	0.5	N
Veronica officinalis	common speedwell, heath speedwell	May-Aug	2"	creeping perennial, spikes of blue fls; dry grassy places	0.05	N

CLIMBERS

Botanical name	Common name	Flowers	Height ft	Notes	Height m	Value
Celastrus	climbing bittersweet	Jun on	20-30	yellow and red pea-sized fruits; well-drained but moist soil, no chalk, shelter from NE winds	6.1-9.1	N
Clematis armandii		Apr-May	30	ev, white and pale pink fls; suits alkaline soil, shade base of stem and roots	9.1	P
C. montana		Apr-May	40	white/pink fls; suits alkaline soil, trellis/posts/old tree stumps	12.2	N P
Eccremocarpus scaber	Chilean glory flower	Jul on	8-10	orange/yellow/red tubular fls; loamy well-drained soil, S/SW walls/trellis/wires	2.4-3.0	N B
Hedera helix	common ivy	Sep-Dec	50-100	ev; any soil type, sun/shade	15.2-30.5	N P B
Hydrangea petiolaris	Japanese climbing hydrangea	Jun	<60	flat white fl heads; moist loamy soil, sun/pt shade	<18.3	N
Parthenocissus quinquefolia	Virginia creeper	Aug	<70	crimson lvs in autumn, self-clinging; loamy moist soil	<21.3	N P B
Passiflora caerulea	passion flower	Jun-Sep	20-30	very attractive whitish fls with purple-blue corona; ordinary soil, S/W wall, protect from frost when young	6.1-9.1	N P
Schizophragma integrifolium		Jul	15-20	self-clinging; rich loamy moist soil, tolerates shade, mulch in spring	4.6-6.1	N

Solanum crispum	Chilean potato-tree	Jun–Sep	15–20	purple-blue star-shaped fls; ordinary well-drained soil, S/W wall, almost hardy	4.6-6.1	N
Vitis	vine	Jun	<80	nectar freely produced only in warm places; rich loamy moist soil, S/W facing site	<24.4	N P
Wisteria sinensis	Chinese wisteria	May(Aug)	<100	nectar only in warm weather; blue/white/mauve fls; rich moist loam, S/W facing wall, shelter	<30.5	N P B

TREES

Botanical name	Common name	Flowers	Height ft	Notes	Height m	Value
Acer	maple	Apr-Jun		well-drained but moist cool soil, sun/pt shade, shelter spp for autumn colour from prevailing wind		N P
A. campestre	field maple		15-40	lvs yellow and red in autumn	4.6-12.2	N P
A. ginnala	Amur maple		15-20	crimson in autumn	4.6-6.1	N P
A. griseum	paper bark maple		20-40	red autumn lvs, attractive bark	6.1-12.2	N P
A. negundo cvs	box elder		40-60	cvs with variegated/yellow lvs	12.2-18.3	N P
A. palmatum cvs	Japanese maple		10-14	good autumn colour	3.0-4.3	N P
A. platanoides cvs 'Goldsworth Purple'	Norway maple		60-70	lvs yellow in autumn purple/crimson leaves	18.3-21.3	N P
A. pseudoplatanus	sycamore		70-80	lvs yellow in autumn	21.3-24.4	N P B
Aesculus				fertile soil, sun/pt shade		
A. carnea	red horse-chestnut	Apr-Jun	30-50	crimson fls	9.1-15.2	N P
A. hippocastanum	horse-chestnut	Apr-May	80-100	huge panicles of white fls spotted yellow and red	24.4-30.5	N P B
A. indica	Indian horse-chestnut	Apr-Jun	80-100	white fls with pink and yellow flush	24.4-30.5	N P
A. pavia	red buckeye	Jun	12-20	red fls	3.7-6.1	N P

Botanical name	Common name	Flowering	Height	Notes	Range	Codes
Ailanthus altissima	tree of heaven	Jul-Aug	60-90	male and female trees; tolerates city atmosphere	18.3-27.4	N P
Alnus	alder			very good in wet places; catkins provide useful early pollen		P
A. cordata	Italian alder	Mar	60-80	bright green shiny lvs; good on chalk	18.3-24.4	P
A. glutinosa	common alder	Feb-Mar	50-70	blunt lvs with smooth undersides	15.2-21.3	P B
A. incana	grey alder	Feb	60-70	good on cold wet sites	18.3-21.3	P
Betula	birch	May	20-60	some spp very beautiful bark, graceful; acid/neutral soil wide spread surface roots	6.1-18.3	P
Castanea sativa	Spanish chestnut, sweet chestnut	Jul	50-60	fls inconspicuous; good soil, sun	15.2-18.3	N P
Catalpa bignonioides	Indian bean	Jul-Aug	30-50	showy white fls, extra-floral nectaries; good soil, sun, shelter, good in towns	9.1-15.2	N P B
Cercis siliquastrum	Judas tree	May-Jun	12-15	pretty pink pea-like fls; good soil, full sun, shelter from late frosts	3.7-4.6	N P
Crataegus (single cvs)				ordinary soil, open sunny posn, tolerates some shade; most give fls and berries, susceptible to fireblight		N P B
C. crus-galli	cockspur thorn	Jun	15-18	autumn colour	4.6-5.5	N P B
C. monogyna	hawthorn	May	20-30	good in streets or as a specimen	6.1-9.1	N P
C. oxycantha = C. laevigata	Midland hawthorn	May	20-30	neat round-headed tree	6.1-9.1	N P

Botanical name	Common name	Flowers	Height ft	Notes	Height m	Value
C. prunifolia		Jun	15-18	autumn colour and fruits	4.6-5.5	N P
Fagus sylvatica	beech	Apr-May	80-120	short fl season; not on heavy wet soil	24.4-36.6	P
Fraxinus	ash	May	50-70	ordinary soil, sun/pt shade, esp towns/coast	15.2-21.3	P
Garrya eliptica		Feb-Mar	8-15	ev grey-green lvs, greyish male catkins; well-drained soil, shelter	2.4-4.6	P
Ilex aquifolium	common holly	May	40-50	some with variegated foliage; separate male and female plants	12.2-15.2	N P
Koelreuteria paniculata	golden rain tree	Jul-Aug	10-40	yellow fls; loamy soil, full sun	3.0-12.2	N
Liquidambar styraciflua	sweet gum	Mar	50-70	inconspicuous fls, autumn lvs; moist loam, sun/pt shade, shelter	15.2-21.3	N
Liriodendron tulipifera	tulip tree	Jul	60-90	yellow-green fls; well-drained soil, sun/light shade	18.3-27.4	N P
Malus	crab apple	Apr-May	20-40	fruits and fls; ordinary well-drained soil with manure	6.1-12.2	N P B
Nothofagus procera	rauli		<80	autumn colour; not on chalk	<24.4	P
Populus	poplar			good on heavy cold soil, open sunny posn, 60'+ away from buildings		P
P. nigra	black poplar	Mar-Apr	<100		<30.5	P

Species	Common name	Flowering	Height (<50)	Notes	<15.2	Codes
P. tremula	aspen	Feb-Mar	<50	long woolly catkins, trembling lvs	<15.2	P
Prunus				not dry or waterlogged soils, well-drained soil with a trace of lime preferred		N P B
P. avium (single cvs)	wild cherry	Apr	60-70	autumn colour, white spring fls	18.3-21.3	N P B
P. cerasifera	myrobalan plum, cherry plum	Feb-Mar	25-30	very pale pink fls	7.6-9.1	N P B
P. dulcis = P. amygdalus	almond	Feb-Mar	20-25	deep pink fls	6.1-7.6	N P B
P. padus	bird cherry	May	40-60	autumn colour, white fls	12.2-18.3	N P B
P. persica (single cvs)	peach	Apr-May	15-20	pink fls; fruit	4.6-6.1	N P B
P. sargentii	Sargent's cherry	Mar-Apr	25-30	autumn foliage, pink fls	7.6-9.1	N P B
P. serrulata (single/semi-double cvs)	Japanese cherry	Mar-Apr	20	white/pink fls; alkaline soil	6.1	N P B
P. spinosa	blackthorn	Mar-May	12-15	white fls	3.6-4.6	N P B
P. subhirtella	spring cherry	Apr	20-25	pendulous pink/white fls, winter fl cvs also	6.1-7.6	N P B
P. x yedoensis	Yoshino cherry	Apr	25-30	earliest Japanese cherry, pink/white fls	7.6-9.1	N P B
Quercus	oak	May	40-80	short flowering season; ordinary well-drained soil, open posn, full sun	12.2-24.4	P

Botanical name	Common name	Flowers	Height ft	Notes	Height m	Value
Robinia pseudoacacia	false acacia	Jun	60-80	scented cream fls; ordinary well-drained soil, some shelter, good town tree	18.3-24.4	N P B
Salix	willow			moist soil, sun, useful by ponds streams etc		
S. alba	white willow	Apr-May	70-80	narrow silvery silky lvs	21.3-24.4	N P B
S. fragilis	crack willow	Mar-Apr	70-80	winter stems	21.3-24.4	N P B
S. purpurea 'Pendula'	purple willow	May	15-20	linear bluish-green lvs purple bark	4.6-6.1	N P B
Sorbus				ordinary well-drained soil, sun/pt shade, good in towns		
S. aria	white beam	May	30-40	white backs to lvs, white-cream fls, berries	9.1-12.2	N P
S. aucuparia	mountain ash	May-Jun	30-50	white fls, red berries early	9.1-15.2	N P B
S. hupehensis	hupeh rowan	Jun	<40	white/very pale pink berries	<12.2	N P
S. intermedia	Swedish whitebeam	May	<40	good in towns	<12.2	N
Tilia x euchlora	Crimea lime	Jun-Aug	50-60	moist but well-drained soil, good in towns, less honeydew than some	15.2-18.3	N P B
Ulmus	elm	Feb-Mar	40-100	subject to branch dropping and Dutch elm disease; ordinary soil, sunny posn	12.2-30.5	P

SHRUBS

Botanical name	Common name	Flowers	Height ft	Notes	Height m	Value
Amelanchier	snowy mespilus	Apr	20-30	white fls, autumn foliage; good moist soil, sun/pt shade	6.1-9.1	P
Aralia elata	Japanese angelica tree	Aug-Sep	<30	large handsome lvs; good soil, sun/shade, hardy in S, shelter elsewhere	<9.1	N
Arbutus unedo	strawberry tree	Oct-Nov	15-25	ev, red frs & fls together if mild; lime-free loam, sun shelter, hardy in S	4.6-7.6	N P
Berberis	barberry			not in USA because of black rust; all tolerate poor soil, sun/pt shade, easy to grow		
B. darwinii		Apr-May	8-10	ev, yellow/orange fls, blue berries; good for hedging	2.4-3.0	N P B
B. prattii		Apr-May	6-8	red berries	1.8-2.4	N P B
B. x stenophylla 'Irwinii'		Apr-May	2	spreading ev, deep gold fls	0.6	N P B
B. thunbergii		Apr-May	6-8	autumn colour, yellow fls, scarlet berries; good for hedging	1.8-2.4	N P B
B. thunbergii 'Atropurpurea'		Apr-May	5-6½	rich bronze-red lvs, autumn colour; good for hedging	1.5-2.0	N P B
B. wilsoniae		Jul	3-4	semi-prostrate, red berries; ground cover on banks	0.9-1.2	N P B

Botanical name	Common name	Flowers	Height ft	Notes	Height m	Value
Buddleia davidii	butterfly bush	May-Aug	12-15	fls purple plumes; loam, tolerates lime, full sun	3.7-4.6	N B
B. globosa	orange ball tree	May-Aug	12-15	semi-ev, fls golden balls; loam, tolerates lime, full sun, wall-shelter as not fully hardy	3.7-4.6	N B
Buxus sempervirens	common box	Apr	15-18	ev, inconspicuous fls; ordinary soil, sun/pt shade, hedging/edging/topiary	4.6-5.5	N P
Calluna vulgaris	ling, heather	Aug-Sep	1-2	ev, white/pink/purple fls; moist acid, peaty soil, sun, clear away fallen lvs	0.3-0.6	N P B
Caragana arborescens	pea tree	May	15-25	yellow pea-like fls; poor soil, not very hardy	4.6-7.6	N P B
Ceanothus (spring fl spp)		Mar	20-25	some ev, blue fls; light soil with low lime content, S or W wall	6.1-7.6	N P B
Chaenomeles speciosa (single cvs)	Japanese quince	Mar-Apr	3-4/ 10-12	pink/white/scarlet/orange fls; ordinary soil, sun, wall shrub	0.9-1.2/ 3.0-3.7	N P B
Cistus	rock-rose, sun rose	May-Jul	2-2½/ 6-8	single white/pink fls; poor well-drained soil, full sun, shelter, hardy in S	0.6-0.8/ 1.8-2.4	N P B
Colutea arborescens	bladder senna	Jun-Sep	4-5	yellow fls, swollen pods; ordinary soil, sun	1.2-1.5	N P B
Cornus alba	dogwood	May-Jun	8-10	winter stems, if pruned too hard no fls; fertile soil, sun/pt shade	2.4-3.0	N P

Botanical name	Common name	Flowering	Height	Description	pH	N P B
C. mas	cornelian cherry	Feb-Mar	15-20	small yellow fls; moist soil, sun/pt shade	4.6-6.1	N P B
C. stolonifera	red osia dogwood	May-Jun	6-8	coloured stems as above; moist soil, sun/pt shade	1.8-2.4	N
Cotinus coggygria = Rhus cotinus	smoke tree	Jun-Jul	12-16	fl stalks and autumn colour fls minute; ordinary well-drained soil, sun	3.7-4.9	N
C. coggygria 'Foliis Purpureis'		Jun-Jul	10-12	plum-purple foliage, autumn colour	3.0-3.7	N
Cotoneaster				all easily grown, ordinary soil, sun, susceptable to fire blight		
C. conspicuus		Jun	3-4	spreading ev, white fls, red berries	0.9-1.2	N P B
C. x 'Cornubia'		Jun	15-20	semi-ev, cream fls, red fruits; screening	4.6-6.1	N P B
C. dammeri		Jun	1"-2"	prostrate, spreading ev, white fls, red berries; ground cover/banks	0.03-0.05	N P B
C. franchetii		Jul	8-12	ev, white/pink fls, orange-red berries; hedging	2.4-3.7	N P B
C. frigidus		Jun-Jul	15-25	semi-ev, white fls, red berries	4.6-7.6	N P B
C. horizontalis		May	2½-4	spreading, small pink fls, red berries; banks/rocks/walls	0.8-1.2	N P B
C. microphyllus		May-Jun	2½-4	ev, white fls, scarlet berries; ground cover/against walls	0.8-1.2	N P B
C. salicifolius 'Rugosus'		Jun	15-20	ev, white fls, red berries	4.6-6.1	N P B

43

44

Botanical name	Common name	Flowers	Height ft	Notes	Height m	Value
C. simonsii		Jun	10-12	semi-ev, white fls, red berries; informal hedging	3.0-3.7	N P B
Cytisus	broom	May-Jun	½ / 6-7	fls white/yellow/pink/orange; ordinary/poor well-drained soil, full sun	0.15/ 1.8-2.1	N P B
Daphne cneorum	garland flower	Apr-May	1-1½	prostrate ev, scented pink fls; ordinary well-drained soil with some chalk, sun/pt shade	0.3-0.5	N P
D. mezereum	mezereon	Feb-Mar	3½-4½	scented pink/mauve/violet/white fls; not long lived	1.1-1.4	N P
Deutzia x kalmiiflora		May-Jun	4-5	very pale pink fls; ordinary well-drained soil, sun/pt shade, some shelter	1.2-1.5	P
D. scabra		Jun-Jul	8-12	attractive bark, white fls; ordinary soil, full sun/light woodland conditions	2.4-3.7	P
Diervilla		May-Jun	6-8	showy fls; well-drained but moist soil, sun/pt shade	1.8-2.4	N
Elaeagnus pungens		Oct-Nov	9-12	spreading ev, some variegated, white inconspicuous fls; poor/ordinary soil, tolerates chalk, hedging, good by sea	2.7-3.7	B
Erica erigena = E. mediterranea		Mar-Apr	5-7	ev, white/pink/purple fls; peaty soil, tolerates chalk if not too dry	1.5-2.1	N P B
E. herbacea	winter heath	Nov-Apr	<1	ev, white/pink fls; peaty soil, tolerates chalk, moisture, sun, open posn	<0.3	N P B

Name	Common name	Flowering	Height	Description	Spread	Type
E. tetralix	cross-leaved heath	Jun-Oct	½-1	ordinary non-limey soil, also boggy soil	0.15-0.3	N P B
E. vagans	Cornish heath	Sep-Nov	1½-2	ev, white/pink/red fls; tolerates mildly alkaline soil	0.5-0.6	N P B
Escallonia hybrids 'Donard Seedling' 'Donard Star'		Jun	9-12	ev, pink fls; ordinary well-drained soil, lime tolerant, shelter in cold gardens	2.7-3.7	N B
Euonymus alatus	winged spindle tree	May-Jun	6-8	autumn colour and fruits; ordinary soil, sun/pt shade	1.8-2.4	N
Fuchsia		Jun-Oct	4-8	purple/scarlet/white/pink fls; ordinary soil with humus, fully hardy only in mild areas	1.8-2.4	N P B
Genista				ordinary well-drained soil, full sun		
G. aetnensis	Mount Etna broom	Jul	15-20	pale yellow fls	4.6-6.1	B
G. hispanica	Spanish gorse	May-Jun	2½-4	spiny spreading branches, golden fls; hardy only in S	0.8-1.2	B
G. lydia		May-Jun	2½-3	spreading/prostrate branches, yellow fls; banks/walls etc	0.8-0.9	B
G. tinctoria		Jul	2½	rich golden-yellow fls	0.8	B
Hamamelis japonica	Japanese witch hazel	Dec-Feb	12-18	yellow winter fls; neutral-acid soil, moisture, sun, some shelter	3.7-5.5	P
H. mollis	Chinese witch hazel	Dec-Feb	12-18	felted lvs, autumn colour, scented yellow fls	3.7-5.5	P

Botanical name	Common name	Flowers	Height ft	Notes	Height m	Value
Hebe		May-Sep	½-6	ev lvs, attractive fls; tolerates chalk, sun, good on coast	0.15-1.8	N B
H. pinguifolia 'Pagei'		May-Jun	<1	ev grey lvs, white fls; well-drained soil, tolerates chalk, sun, ground cover	<0.3	N B
H. salicifolia		Jul-Aug	5-10	racemes of white fls; well-drained soil, tolerates chalk, full sun, shelter, semi-hardy	1.5-3.0	N B
Hippophae rhamnoides	sea buckthorn	Apr	15-25	male & female plants, fls inconspicuous, orange berries; well-drained/sandy soil, sun/pt shade, good on coast	4.6-7.6	B
Hydrangea		Aug-Sep	6-8	many shades white/pink/blue fls; moist fertile soil, sun/pt shade, shelter from spring frost	1.8-2.4	N P
Hypericum	tutsan	Jun-Aug	3½-4½	yellow fls; pt shade, good by sea	1.1-1.4	P B
H. calycinum	rose-of-Sharon	Jun-Aug	1-1½	spreads widely, yellow fls; fertile well-drained soil, dry shade but fls best in sun	0.3-0.5	P B
H. 'Hidcote'		Jul-Sep	3-6	semi-ev, yellow fls; fertile well-drained soil, sun	0.9-1.8	P B
Kolkwitzia amabilis	beauty bush	May-Jun	6-8	pink fls; well-drained soil, full sun	1.8-2.4	B
Laurus nobilis	bay laurel	May-Jun	10-18	culinary value; ordinary soil, sun, shelter,	3.0-5.5	N B

Lavandula	lavender	Jul-Aug	<3	ev aromatic lvs, fragrant blue/lavender/purple fls; well-drained soil, sun, hedging	<0.9	N P B
L. 'Hidcote'		Jul-Aug	1½	short dark violet fls	0.5	B
Ligustrum ovalifolium	privet	Jul	6-8	semi-ev, cream fls; ordinary soil, sun/shade	1.8-2.4	N P B
Lonicera x purpursii	winter-flowering honeysuckle	Dec-Feb	7-9	white scented fls; well-drained soil with humus, sun/pt shade	2.1-2.7	N P
L. standishii		Jan-Feb	7-9	cream/white fls freely produced	2.1-2.7	N P
Magnolia				well-drained loamy soil, shelter N/E wind, mulch with peat etc		
M. denudata	yulan	May	25-30	white fls	7.6-9.1	P
M. grandiflora	bull bay	Jul-Sep	30-40	ev, scented fls, best by wall	9.1-12.2	P
M. kobus		Apr	25-30	white fls; tolerates lime	7.6-9.1	P
M. x soulangiana		Apr-May	20-30	white and pink fls, purple forms	6.1-9.1	P B
M. stellata		Mar-Apr	10-15	starry white fls	3.0-4.6	P B
Mahonia aquifolium	Oregon grape	Feb-May	3-5	ev, yellow fls; fertile moist soil, sun/pt shade, ground cover, very hardy	0.9-1.5	N P B
M. japonica		Feb-Mar	5-7	ev handsome foliage, yellow scented fls; fertile moist soil with humus, light shade	1.5-2.1	N P B
Mespilus germanica	medlar	May-Jun	20-25	outstanding white fls, fr edible; well-drained soil, open posn, sun, spring mulch	6.1-7.6	N P B

Botanical name	Common name	Flowers	Height ft	Notes	Height m	Value
Olearia x haastii	daisy bush	Jul-Aug	6-9	ev, white daisy fls; well-drained loam, sun, good in towns/coast	1.8-2.7	N P B
Osmanthus delavayi		Apr	7-10	ev, scented white fls; well-drained soil, sun/pt shade, shelter	2.1-3.0	
O. heterophyllus = O. ilicifolius		Sep-Oct	7-9	ev, white scented fls; well-drained soil, sun/pt shade, shelter, hedging	2.1-2.7	
Perovskia atriplicifolia		Aug-Sep	6-8	grey upright stems, blue fls; light soil, sun, cut down to 1' in spring, not long lived	1.8-2.4	N
Philadelphus	mock orange	Jun-Jul	3½-4½/9-12	white scented fls; ordinary well-drained soil, sun/pt shade	1.1-1.4/2.7-3.7	N P B
Photinia villosa		May	12-18	berries and red lvs in autumn	3.7-5.5	
Potentilla fruticosa	shrubby cinquefoil	May-Aug	3½-4	many cvs, fls white/yellow/orange/scarlet; light well-drained soil, full sun	1.1-1.2	N P B
P. fruticosa 'Arbuscula'		Jun-Oct	2	rich yellow fls; light well-drained soil, full sun	0.6	N P B
Prunus laurocerasus	cherry laurel	Apr	15-20	ev, white fls; ordinary soil with some lime, tolerates shade, screens etc, extra-floral nectar at other times	4.6-6.1	N P

Species	Common name	Flowering	Height	Description	Spacing	Uses
P. lusitanica	Portugal laurel	Jun	10-15	ev large lvs, cream fls; ordinary soil with some lime, tolerates shade, hedging	3.0-4.6	N P
Pyracantha	firethorn	May-Jun	14-16	ev, yellow/orange berries; fertile well-drained soil, tolerates chalk, sun/pt shade	4.3-4.9	N P B
Rhamnus catharticus	common buckthorn	May	6-8	very small green fls, black berries; chalk	1.8-2.4	N P
R. frangula = Frangula alnus	alder buckthorn	May	6-8	red/black berries	1.8-2.4	N P
Rhus glabra	smooth sumach	Jul-Aug	4-6	autumn foliage; ordinary soil, sun	1.2-1.8	N P
R. typhina	stag's horn sumach	Jul	10-15	autumn foliage, hairy young shoots; ordinary soil, sun	3.0-4.6	N P
Ribes sanguineum	flowering currant	Mar-Apr	8-10	pink fls; ordinary well-drained soil, sun/pt shade, annual mulch	2.4-3.0	N P B
R. speciosum		May-Jun	8-10	red fls; ordinary well-drained soil, sun/pt shade, annual mulch	2.4-3.0	N P B
Rosa (single cvs)		May-Sep		many spp; well-drained soil with compost/manure, sun		P B
R. rugosa	Ramanas rose	Jun-Jul	5-8	fragrant purple/white fls	1.5-2.4	P B
Rosmarinus officinalis	rosemary	Apr-May	6-7	ev aromatic lvs, blue fls; ordinary well-drained soil, sun	1.8-2.1	N P B
Rubus deliciosus		May-Jun	6-10	large white fls, ordinary well-drained soil, sun/pt shade	1.8-3.0	N P
R. odoratus	thimble berry	Jul-Sep	6-8	rose-pink fls; ordinary well-drained soil, sun/pt shade	1.8-2.4	N P

Botanical name	Common name	Flowers	Height ft	Notes	Height m	Value
Salix aegyptiaca = S. medemii		Jan-Feb	12-14	showy early male plants; moist soil, sun	3.7-4.3	N P B
S. caprea	goat willow, sallow	Feb-Mar	15-20	silver-grey male catkins; woodland/hedgerows	4.6-6.1	N P B
S. repens	creeping willow	Apr	4-7	silver-grey male catkins; moist soil, sun, ground cover etc	1.2-2.1	N P B
S. x smithiana		Mar-Apr	15	moist soil, sun	4.6	N P B
Senecio greyi		Jun-Jul	4-5	grey lvs, yellow fls; ordinary well-drained soil, sun, good on coast	1.2-1.5	P B
Skimmia japonica		Mar	1½-2	ev, berries on male plants; ordinary well-drained soil, sun/pt shade	0.5-0.6	N P
Staphylea	bladdernut	May-Jun	7	panicles of white fls, interesting fruit	2.1	N P
Symphoricarpos	snowberry	Jun-Jul	5-8	spreads by suckers, white/pink berries; ordinary well-drained soil, sun/pt shade	1.5-2.4	N P B
Syringa	lilac	May	15-18	white/pink/mauve fls; fertile soil, sun/pt shade, hedges/ screens	4.6-5.5	P
Tamarix pentandra	tamarisk	Jul-Aug	12-15	feathery heads of pink fls; well-drained lime-free soil, sun, windbreaks/hedges on coast	3.7-4.6	N P

Botanical name	Common name	Flowering		Description	Height	Propagation
Ulex europaeus	common gorse	Apr-May	4-5	spiny ev, yellow fls; poor/ordinary well-drained soil, full sun	1.2-1.5	N P B
U. minor = U. nanus	dwarf gorse	Sep	$\frac{1}{2}$-1	spiny ev, yellow fls; poor/ordinary well-drained soil, full sun	0.15-0.3	N P B
Viburnum				good moist soil, sun, shelter early flowering cvs from frost		
V. opulus	guelder rose	May-Jun	10-15	white fls	3.0-4.6	N
V. plicatum 'Tomentosum' = V. tomentosum		May	9-12	white fls	2.7-3.7	N P
V. tinus	laurustinus	Jan-Apr	7-10	ev, buds pink, fls white	2.1-3.0	P
Weigela florida and hybrids		May-Jun	6-8	showy pink/white/red fls; good moist but well-drained soil, sun/pt/shade	1.8-2.4	N B
Yucca filamentosa	Adam's needle	Sep	2-2$\frac{1}{2}$	ev erect spine-tipped lvs, cream fls in panicles; well-drained soil, full sun	0.6-0.8	P B

READING LIST

1. Alford, D.V. (1975)   Bumblebees.   London, UK : Davis-Poynter 352 pages

2. Crane, E. (1980)   A book of honey.   Oxford, UK : Oxford University Press   198 pages

3. ___ (1981)   Wild gardens for bees.   Bee Wld 4 : 128-129   IBRA Research News No. 17

4. Gleim, K.-H. (1977)   Nahrungsquellen des Bienenvolkes.   [Food sources of the honeybee colony.]   St Augustine, German Federal Republic : Delta Verlag   159 pages

5. Hensels, L.G.M. (1981)   Drachtplantengids voor de bijenteelt. [Guide to bee forage plants.]   Wageningen, Netherlands: Centre for Agricultural Publishing and Documentation   126 pages

6. Hodges, D. (1978)   A calendar of bee plants.   Bee Wld 59(3) : 97-100   IBRA Reprint M94

7. ___ (1974)   The pollen loads of the honeybee: a guide to their identification by colour and form.   London, UK : International Bee Research Association   114 pages

8. Howes, F.N. (1979)   Plants and beekeeping.   London, UK : Faber & Faber rev. ed.   256 pages

9. Louveaux, J. (1980)   Les abeilles et leur elevage. [Bees and beekeeping.]   Paris : Librairie Hachette   235 pages

10. Maurizio, A. & Grafl, I. (1980)   Das Trachtpflanzenbuch. Nektar und Pollen - die wichtigsten Nahrungsquellen der Honigbiene. [Book of bee plants. Nectar and pollen - the most important food sources of the honeybee.]   Munich, German Federal Republic : Ehrenwirth Verlag

11. Nature Conservancy Council & Botanical Society of the British Isles (1981)   Growing wild flowers from seed.   1-page leaflet

12. Pellett, F.C. (1976)   American honey plants.   Hamiliton, IL, USA : Dadant & Sons   (facsimile of 1947 ed.)   467 pages

13. Ricciardelli d'Albore, G. & Persano Oddo, L. (1978)   Flora apistica italiana.   [Italian bee forage.]   Florence, Italy : Istituto Sperimentale per la Zoologia Agraria   286 pages

All except item 11 can be purchased from IBRA (address on page 2); publications lists will be sent on request.   Item 11 is available from BSBI, White Cottage, Slinfold, Horsham, West Sussex RH13 7RG (send a stamped addressed envelope or International Reply Coupon)

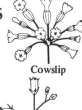